To:

_____

From:

_____

Date:

_____

ZONDERKIDZ

The Beginner's Bible® Activity Book
Copyright © 2012 by Zondervan
Illustrations © 2012 by Zondervan

Requests for information should be addressed to:

Zonderkidz, 3900 *Sparks Drive SE, Grand Rapids, Michigan* 49546

ISBN 978-0-310-75979-9

Illustrator: Denis Alonso
Art direction and cover design: Cindy Davis

Printed in the United States

18 19 20 21 22 23 24 25 /LSC/ 14 13 12 11 10 9 8 7 6 5 4 3 2

Activity Book

ZONDERkidz
.com

Creation

Searching
Find and circle the words in the puzzle below.

BIRD   **FISH**   **OCEAN**

SKY   **WATER**

F W A T E R

I K P N O P

S O C E A N

H R L V D S

X Z Q M J K

B I R D F Y

5

Trace the Numbers

Adam named the animals one by one. Trace the numbers.

Where Is Eve?

Help Adam find Eve.

Color the Garden

God made a beautiful garden for Adam and Eve. Color the apples red. Color the leaves and grass green. Color the trunks brown. Use your favorite colors to color the flowers.

Noah's Ark

Noah built an ark which took work and practice.
Practice tracing the lines below.

Practice tracing lines top to bottom.

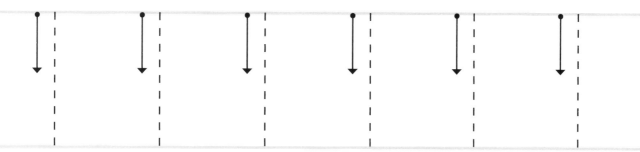

Practice tracing lines left to right.

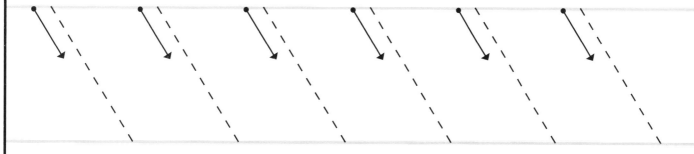

Practice tracing circles.

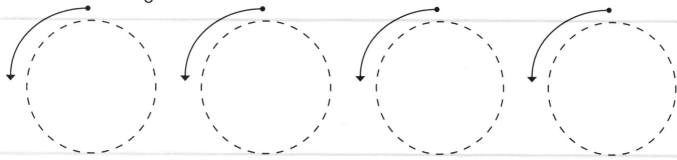

Noah Does It

God said, "Take your family and two of every animal into the ark."
Trace the 2. Color two of each creature.

Rainbow Bright

God put a beautiful rainbow in the sky.

Twelve Sons

Joseph was one of Jacob's 12 sons. Count the brothers. Trace the numbers.

1 2 3 4 5 6

7 8 9 10 11 12

Coat of Many Colors

Joseph had a colorful robe. Color Joseph's robe.

Joseph Helps

Joseph is wise. Find and circle the words in the puzzle below.

JAIL   **COW**   **DREAM**
LESS   **SKINNY**   **CORN**

```
G  C  A  N  P  E  S  S
B  L  R  U  G  R  K  O
V  O  S  F  I  O  I  I
C  O  W  S  D  M  N  W
N  N  S  R  E  F  N  F
P  I  E  W  W  L  Y  B
X  A  P  R  R  E  V  D
M  L  I  A  J  I  M  L
```

Save Moses

Miriam was afraid. She put Moses in a basket.
Trace ovals. Trace a basket. Draw baby Moses inside.

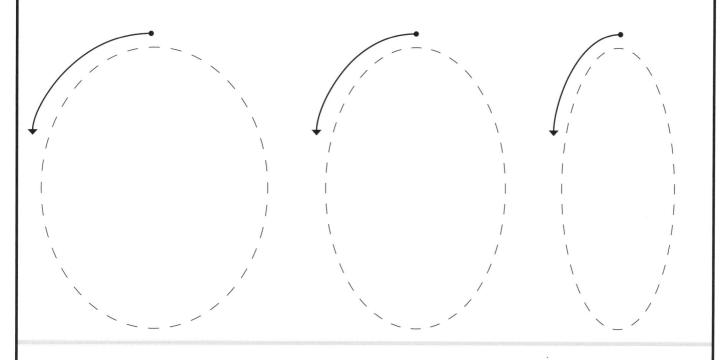

On Fire

Moses saw a burning bush.
Use red, yellow, and orange crayons to draw the flames.

NO!

Pharaoh said, "NO!" Trace N. Trace O. Trace and write NO.

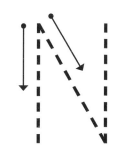 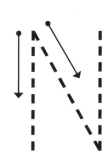 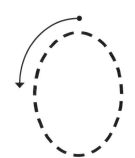 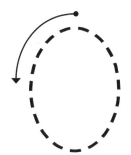

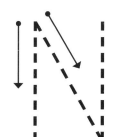 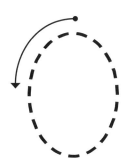 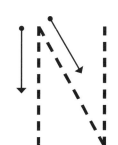 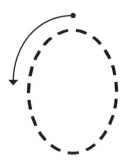

Count to Ten

God sent ten plagues. Trace 10. Circle groups of ten.

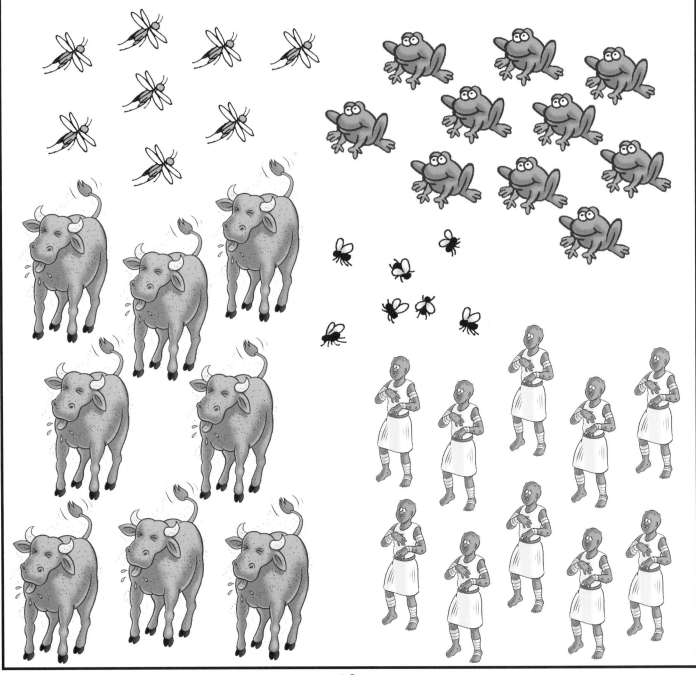

GO!

Finally, Pharaoh said, "GO!" Color the pictures that rhyme with GO.

GO!

PIG

CAKE

FOE

DOUGH

Listen for S

The people were free. They sang praises to God!
Circle the two pictures that begin with the S sound.

sing

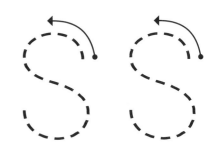 **sandal**

 **crab**

 **sea**

 **donkey**

Ten Rules

God wrote the Ten Commandments for the people to obey.
Trace the numbers. Count backwards from ten.

Same or Different

"I will go wherever you go," Ruth said.
Make an X on the pictures that are the same.

Next?

God said, "I look at the inside of a person. I look at the heart."
Color the hearts and the one that comes next in the pattern.
Use the code to color the hearts: 1= pink, 2 = red, 3 = purple

The Smallest

David was the smallest brother.
Circle the picture that is smaller than the first one.

Big, Bigger, Biggest

Goliath was much bigger than David!
Circle the picture that is bigger than the first one.

25

Which One?

David said, "God will be with me."
Find and circle the stone that hit the giant's forehead.
Color the picture.

Sing Praise

David wrote songs about God called psalms. He wrote,
"The Lord is my shepherd." Look at the picture. Put an X on the
shepherd. Circle some things people need to live. Color the grass green.
Color the water blue.

God Is Good

"The Lord is my shepherd. God's goodness and love will
follow me all the days of my life."
Trace the path from the lamb to David.

Obey and Pray

Daniel prayed to God, not to the king. Draw a picture of your prayer to God.

My prayer.

Trace the Ls

The king threw Daniel in the lions' den. God sent an angel to protect Daniel. Trace and write L. Circle the pictures whose names begin with the L sound like lion.

Lamp

Moon

Rug

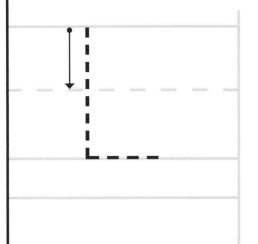

Lion

Legs

Logs

Jonah's Search

Jonah tried to run away from God. He got on a boat.
Find and circle the words in the puzzle below.

SINK   STORM   STOP

SAIL   SEA   SAILOR

```
M  J  N  X  V  V  K  N
X  R  H  N  T  N  N  P
S  T  O  P  E  A  I  G
W  B  P  T  F  L  S  L
J  Z  M  N  S  T  I  E
S  R  O  L  I  A  S  A
V  E  J  W  S  P  P  Y
Z  C  A  R  B  Q  B  C
```

31

God Is Good

God loved Mary and Joseph. God loves you. Connect the dots.

Let's Go To Bethlehem

Mary and Joseph went to Bethlehem. Trace their path.

Jesus Is Here

Jesus is born! Trace and write J. Trace Jesus. Color the picture.

J J J J J

J E S U S

Makes a Difference

Anna and Simeon knew Jesus was the Savior. They could tell
Jesus was different. Circle the pictures that are different from the first one.

Stars

The special star in the sky was a sign from God.
Trace and color the stars. Circle the number of stars.

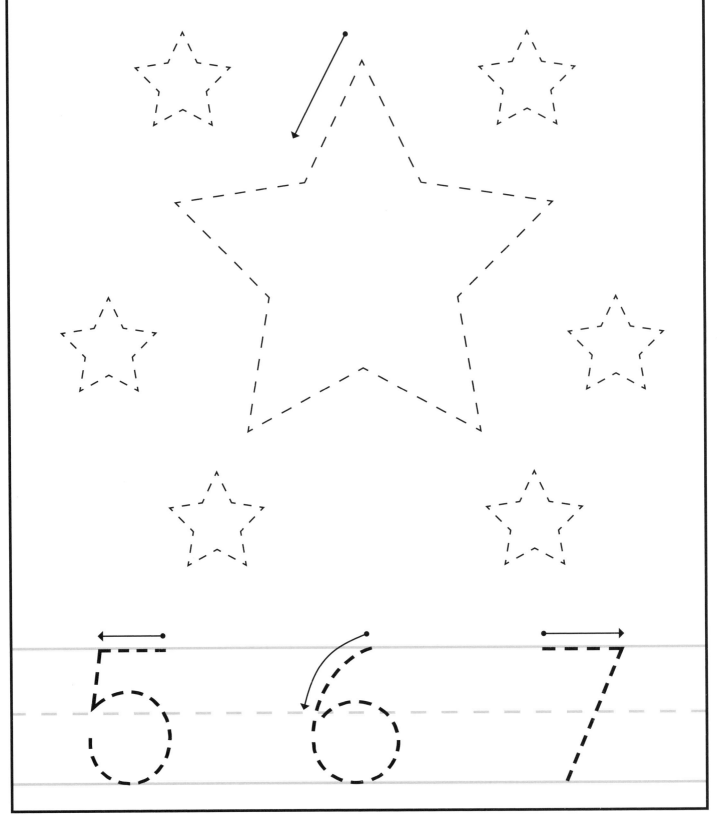

Beside Him

Jesus stood beside the river. He asked John to baptize him.
Follow the directions below to show **beside**. Use a check (✔).

Put a check on Jesus **beside** the river.

Put a check on the person **beside** Joseph.

Put a check on what is **beside** the tree.

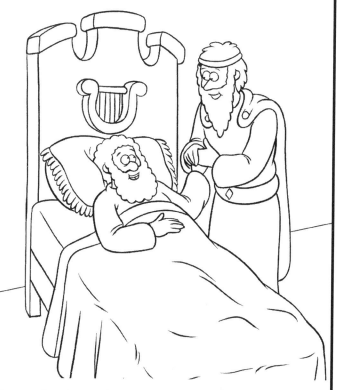

Put a check on the man who is **beside** the bed.

6 + 6 = 12

Jesus chose 12 disciples.
Count the disciples. Circle groups of 6. Trace the numbers.

JESUS

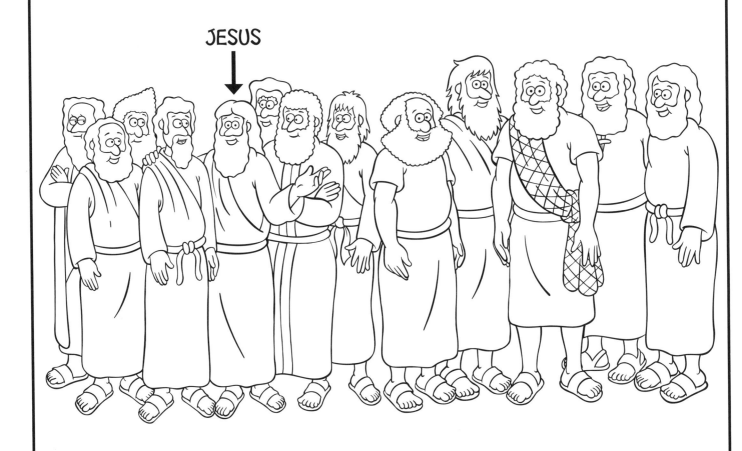

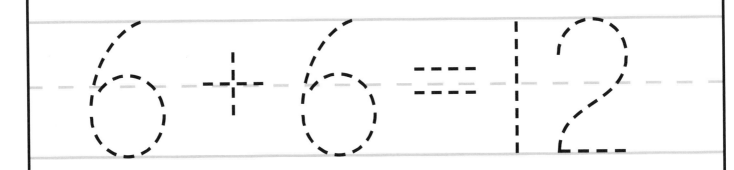

Jesus Teaches

Jesus taught many people. Color the page.

Pray

Jesus taught the people how to pray. Trace and color
the frame for Jesus' prayer.

Our Father in heaven,

hallowed be your name,

your kingdom come,

your will be done

on earth as it is in heaven.

Give us today our daily bread.

Forgive us our debts,

as we also forgive our debtors.

And lead us not into temptation,

but deliver us from the evil one.

Amen

Touching

When the woman touched Jesus, she was well. When Jesus touched the little girl, she was well. Circle the things you can touch.

Sharing

The people were hungry. A boy shared his lunch of five loaves of bread and two small fish. Circle five loaves and two small fish.

How Many?

Read the questions. Jesus told the people a story or parable.
Write the number of how many.

1. How many children? $\quad$ 1 $\quad$ 2 $\quad$ 3

2. How many women? $\quad$ 2 $\quad$ 3 $\quad$ 4

3. How many men? $\quad$ 7 $\quad$ 8 $\quad$ 9

4. How many pets? $\quad$ 1 $\quad$ 2 $\quad$ 3

Missing Number

A shepherd watches over his sheep. He counts them.
Look at each row. Which number is missing? Write the missing number.

1   2   [ ]   4   5

3   [ ]   5   6   7

4   5   6   [ ]   8

6   7   [ ]   9   10

The Lost Sheep

The shepherd looks everywhere for the lost sheep. He does not give up.
Help the shepherd find the lost sheep.

G is for Good

The brother was hungry. The pig's food looked good! Good begins with G. Circle the pictures with the same beginning sound as *good*.

Rock

Goblet

Grain

Gecko

Girl

Stool

Mouse

Blessings Left and Right

Jesus blessed the children on the left and on the right. Draw a left arrow (←) on the children to the left of Jesus. Draw a right arrow (→) on the children to the right of Jesus.

Remember to Say Thanks

"Thank you!" the man said to Jesus.
Thank Jesus for one of his gifts. Draw a picture of that gift.

Thank You, Jesus.

Honor the Lord

Jesus said, "Mary did what was right. She honored me."
Use the code to color the page.

M = orange; J = purple; G = green; B = brown; S = blue; Y = yellow

Jesus' Words

Jesus gave the bread to his disciples. "This bread is my body,"
Jesus told the disciples. "Every time you eat it, think of me."
Find and circle the words in the puzzle below.

BREAD   **BLESSED**   **BROKE**

BLOOD   **BODY**   **BELONG**

E V Y I N C P B

B R E A D B Z L

R K R E D E G E

O T B O J L P S

K B O D Y O P S

E L V F J N L E

B S Q I V G M D

What Next, Jesus?

Jesus took a cup of wine. "This is my blood. It is poured out to forgive the sins of many." Circle what comes next in the pattern.

Jesus' Cross Is Heavy

The soldiers made Jesus carry a big wooden cross.
Trace the rectangles. Draw the cross Jesus had to carry.

1st, 2nd, 3rd

Jesus died on the cross. Write **1** below what happened first. Write **2** below what happened next. Write **3** below what happened last.

Yes, He IS

Everyone was sad. But they forgot! Jesus is the Son of God.
Trace and write I, S, IS!

Not Here!

The angel said, "Jesus is not here. He has risen!"
Circle who has risen.

Help with the Message

The women saw Jesus. Jesus said, "Go tell the others."
Run with Mary to tell the others!

Between You and Me

Jesus stood between the disciples so they could touch his hands and feet. Circle the person between the others.

More Believers

Jesus told the disciples to make more disciples.
Draw more disciples. Give them names.

I Am Sorry

Peter said, "Tell Jesus you are sorry for your sins and be baptized."
Draw a picture of something for which you are sorry. It is for Jesus.

Dear Jesus,
    I am sorry. I love you.

Jesus Loves Me

Peter said, "We did not make the man walk. Jesus did it."
Color Jesus. Cut out the picture. Keep it nearby.

A New Heaven and Earth

John saw a new heaven and a new earth.
Color the new heaven and new earth.

A Love Letter

Decorate this love letter to Jesus. Make it colorful and bright.

I
LOVE
JESUS!

Dear God

Color this letter to God. Trace the letters. Sign your name.

Dear God,

I love you with all my heart.

I am your child.

Please help me every day!

Love,

_____

The bestselling Bible storybook of our time—over 5 million sold!

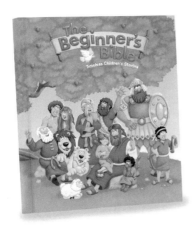

978-0-310-75013-0

$16.99 / Hardcover

The Beginner's Bible® has been a favorite with young children and their parents since its release in 1989 with over 25 million products sold. Now it's redesigned with fresh new art that will excite children for many more years to come.

Full of faith and fun, *The Beginner's Bible*® is a wonderful gift for any child. The easy-to-read text and bright, full-color illustrations on every page make it a perfect way to introduce young children to the stories and characters of the Bible. With new vibrant three-dimensional art and compelling text, more than 90 Bible stories come to life. Kids ages 6 and under will enjoy the fun illustrations of Noah helping the elephant onto the ark, Jonah praying inside the fish, and more, as they discover *The Beginner's Bible*® just like millions of children before. *The Beginner's Bible*® was named the 2006 Retailers Choice Award winner in Children's Nonfiction.

Check out these other products featuring The Beginner's Bible®—

978-0-310-75957-7

978-0-310-76030-6

978-0-310-76111-2

978-0-310-75955-3

978-0-310-75704-7

978-0-310-75701-6

978-0-310-75536-4

978-0-310-75610-1